# SUPERSTARS OF THE STANLEY CUP FINALS

by Brendan Flynn

**Cody Koala**

An Imprint of Pop!

popbooksonline.com

abdopublishing.com

Published by Pop!, a division of ABDO, PO Box 398166, Minneapolis, Minnesota 55439. Copyright © 2019 by POP, LLC. International copyrights reserved in all countries. No part of this book may be reproduced in any form without written permission from the publisher. Pop!™ is a trademark and logo of POP, LLC.

Printed in the United States of America, North Mankato, Minnesota

042018
092018

Cover Photo: Jeanine Leech/Icon SportsWire/AP Images
Interior Photos: Jeanine Leech/Icon SportsWire/AP Images, 1, 6, 9; Mark Humphrey/AP Images, 5 (top), 21; Shutterstock Images, 5 (bottom left), 5 (bottom right); Robin Alam/Icon SportsWire/AP Images, 11, 12; Chris Williams/Icon SportsWire/AP Images, 15; Alex Gallardo/AP Images, 16; John Crouch/Cal Sport Media/AP Images, 19

Editor: Meg Gaertner
Series Designer: Laura Mitchell

Library of Congress Control Number: 2017963427

**Publisher's Cataloging-in-Publication Data**

Names: Flynn, Brendan, author.
Title: Superstars of the Stanley Cup finals / by Brendan Flynn.
Description: Minneapolis, Minnesota : Pop!, 2019. | Series: Sports' greatest superstars | Includes online resources and index.
Identifiers: ISBN 9781532160325 (lib.bdg.) | ISBN 9781532161445 (ebook) |
Subjects: LCSH: Ice hockey players--Juvenile literature. | Sports records--Juvenile literature. | National Hockey League--Juvenile literature.
Classification: DDC 796.9620--dc23

## Hello! My name is

# Cody Koala

Pop open this book and you'll find QR codes like this one, loaded with information, so you can learn even more!

Scan this code* and others like it while you read, or visit the website below to make this book pop.

popbooksonline.com/
superstars-stanley-cup-finals

*Scanning QR codes requires a web-enabled smart device with a QR code reader app and a camera.

# Table of Contents

## Chapter 1

# Sidney Crosby in the Stanley Cup Finals

The Stanley Cup Finals happens every spring. The winning team is the **champion** of the National Hockey League.

Watch a video here!

Sidney Crosby is the **captain** of the Pittsburgh Penguins. He has helped his team win the Stanley Cup three times.

Crosby is one of the top passers in hockey. His teammates love playing with him because his **assists** set them up for so many goals.

Crosby was captain of Canada's Olympic hockey team in 2014.

## Chapter 2

# Patrick Kane

Patrick Kane joined the Chicago Blackhawks in 2007. In the next eight years, Kane helped Chicago win the Stanley Cup three times.

Learn more here!

Kane uses his speed on the ice to skate past the other team. Then he flies in on the **goalie** and shoots. Another goal for Chicago!

## Chapter 3

# Jonathan Quick

Jonathan Quick is one of the best goalies around. He plays for the Los Angeles Kings. He led them to Stanley Cup wins in 2012 and 2014.

Learn more here!

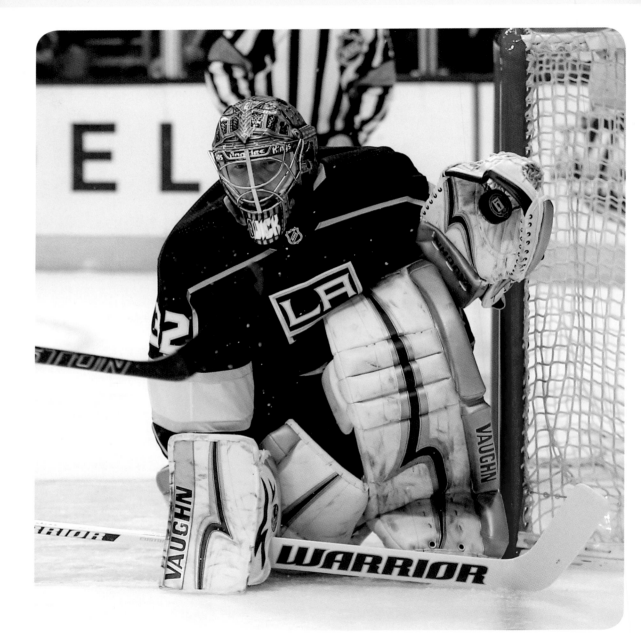

Quick has excellent **reflexes**. When a player shoots the puck at him, he moves very quickly. He does whatever it takes to stop the other team from scoring.

> Quick was a goalie for Team USA in the 2014 Olympics.

## Chapter 4

# Alex Ovechkin

Alex Ovechkin is a **forward** for the Washington Capitals. He scores a lot of goals. He led the NHL in goals seven times in his first 13 seasons.

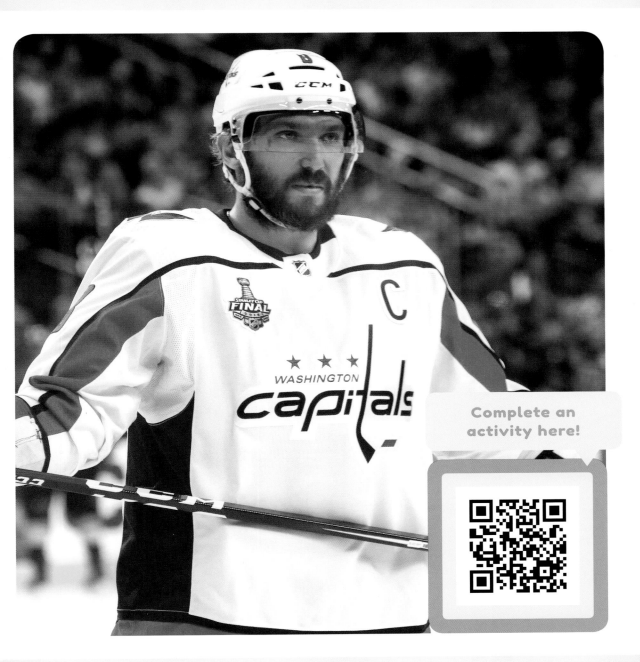

Complete an activity here!

Ovechkin and the Capitals had come close to winning the Stanley Cup many times. But he did not give up. Then they won it in 2018. Ovechkin was finally a champion!

Wayne Gretzky and the Edmonton Oilers win the first of their four Stanley Cups together.

Sidney Crosby leads the Pittsburgh Penguins to two Stanley Cup wins in a row.

**1984**

**2016 and 2017**

**1960**

**2009**

**2012**

The Montreal Canadiens set a record by winning the Stanley Cup five times in a row.

Jonathan Quick leads the Los Angeles Kings to an unexpected Stanley Cup win.

Sidney Crosby wins his first Stanley Cup with the Pittsburgh Penguins.

# Making Connections

## Text-to-Self

Does your school or town have a hockey team? Would you ever want to play hockey? Why or why not?

## Text-to-Text

Have you read about any other great sports players? What makes them so great?

## Text-to-World

Have you ever seen hockey in the news or on television? Why do you think it is so popular?

# Glossary

**assist** – a pass or shot that sets up a teammate to score a goal.

**captain** – the player who is considered the team leader on the ice.

**champion** – the best team in a sport.

**forward** – a skater whose main job is to score goals.

**goalie** – a player who stays around the net and tries to stop the puck from going in.

**reflexes** – being able to react quickly.

# Index

Chicago Blackhawks, 10, 13

forward, 18

goalie, 13, 14, 17

Los Angeles Kings, 14

Pittsburgh Penguins, 7, 18

Washington Capitals, 18, 20